T0023690

# NEWTON'S LAWS OF MOTION FOR SMARTYPANTS

Anushka Ravishankar
Illustrations by Pia Alizé Hazarika

**duckbill**

An imprint of Penguin Random House

DUCKBILL BOOKS

USA | Canada | UK | Ireland | Australia
New Zealand | India | South Africa | China | Singapore

Duckbill Books is part of the Penguin Random House group of companies
whose addresses can be found at global.penguinrandomhouse.com

Published by Penguin Random House India Pvt. Ltd
4th Floor, Capital Tower 1, MG Road,
Gurugram 122 002, Haryana, India

First published in Duckbill Books by
Penguin Random House India 2023

Text copyright © Anushka Ravishankar 2023
Illustrations copyright © Pia Alizé Hazarika 2023

All rights reserved

10 9 8 7 6 5 4 3 2 1

This is a work of non-fiction. The views and opinions expressed in this book are the
author's own and the facts are as reported by her which have been verified to the extent
possible, and the publishers are not in any way liable for the same.

ISBN 9780143461029

Typeset in ArcherPro by DiTech Publishing Services Pvt. Ltd
Printed at Thomson Press India Ltd, New Delhi

This book is sold subject to the condition that it shall not, by way of trade
or otherwise, be lent, resold, hired out, or otherwise circulated without the
publisher's prior consent in any form of binding or cover other than that in
which it is published and without a similar condition including this condition
being imposed on the subsequent purchaser.

www.penguin.co.in

# NEWTON'S LAWS OF MOTION

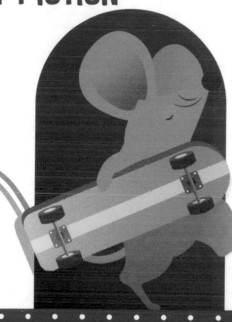

**FIRST LAW:** Any body continues in a state of rest or in uniform motion in a straight line unless acted upon by an external force.

**SECOND LAW:** The net force acting on a body is equal to the product of the mass of the body and the acceleration caused by the force.

**THIRD LAW:** Every action generates an equal and opposite reaction.

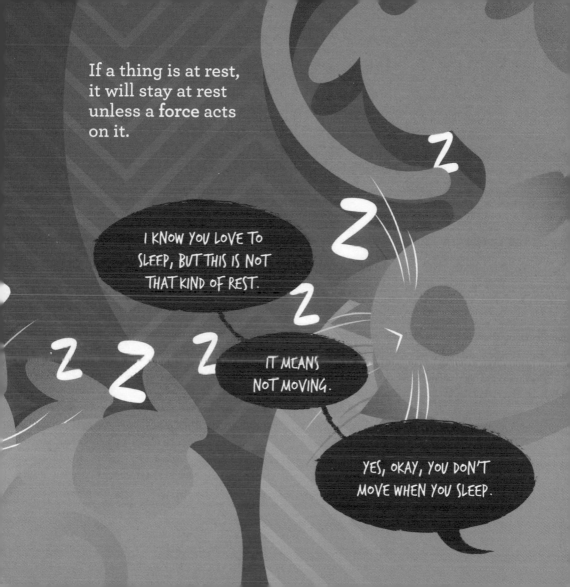

If a thing is at rest, it will stay at rest unless a **force** acts on it.

I KNOW YOU LOVE TO SLEEP, BUT THIS IS NOT THAT KIND OF REST.

IT MEANS NOT MOVING.

YES, OKAY, YOU DON'T MOVE WHEN YOU SLEEP.

When something is at rest, force is needed to make it move.

LIKE ME PUSHING THE MOUSE, YES.

If something is moving in one direction at the same speed, it will keep moving in the same manner unless a force acts on it.

SWAT

FORCE

A force can also change the direction of a moving thing or make it move faster or slower . . .

So a force is needed to change the speed or direction of something that is in motion.

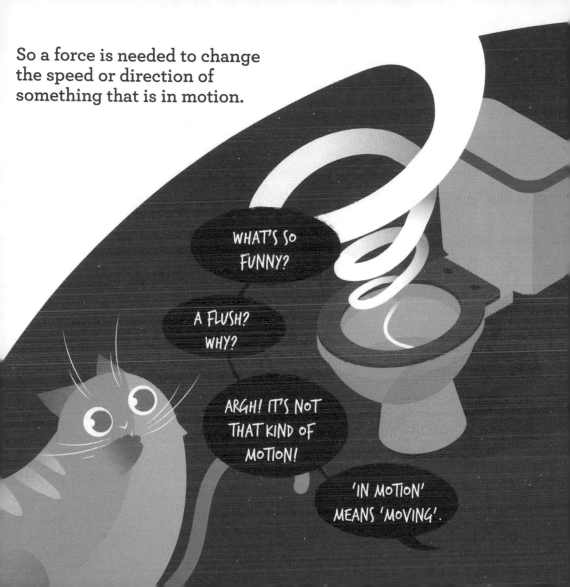

Newton's first law of motion says that a thing that is at rest remains at rest and a thing that is moving at the same speed in a straight line will keep moving unless a force acts on it.

NO, FOOD IS NOT A FORCE.
I KNOW THAT CAN MAKE YOU MOVE REALLY FAST.
SmArtyPanTs

When something moves, it goes fast or slow. How fast or slow it moves in a straight line is called the **speed** of the thing.

WHY IS IT CALLED SPEED?
BECAUSE SOMEONE GAVE
IT THAT NAME.

When something changes speed from less to more or more to less, it is called **acceleration**.

When something changes direction, that is also called acceleration.

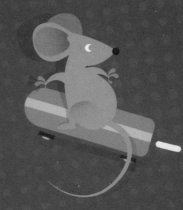

CHANGE IN SPEED

CHANGE IN DIRECTION

NO, YOU CAN'T MAKE UP A NEW WORD FOR IT.
I KNOW IT'S LONG. SO WHAT IF YOU DON'T LIKE IT.
YOU WANT TO CALL IT 'CATATION'?
NO, I DON'T THINK IT'S A BETTER WORD AT ALL.

Matter is what everything
in the world is made of.

Things with more
matter have more mass.

MORE MASS

Mass, acceleration and force are the three things you need to know to understand Newton's second law.

If you want two things to move with the same acceleration, you have to use more force on the bigger one.

THAT'S WHY IT WAS SO HARD FOR YOU TO PUSH THE ELEPHANT.

I DIDN'T SAY YOU'RE WEAK.

MORE FORCE,
MORE ACCELERATION

WHEEEZe

And if you have two things with the same mass,
then the thing that you push with more force
will move faster.

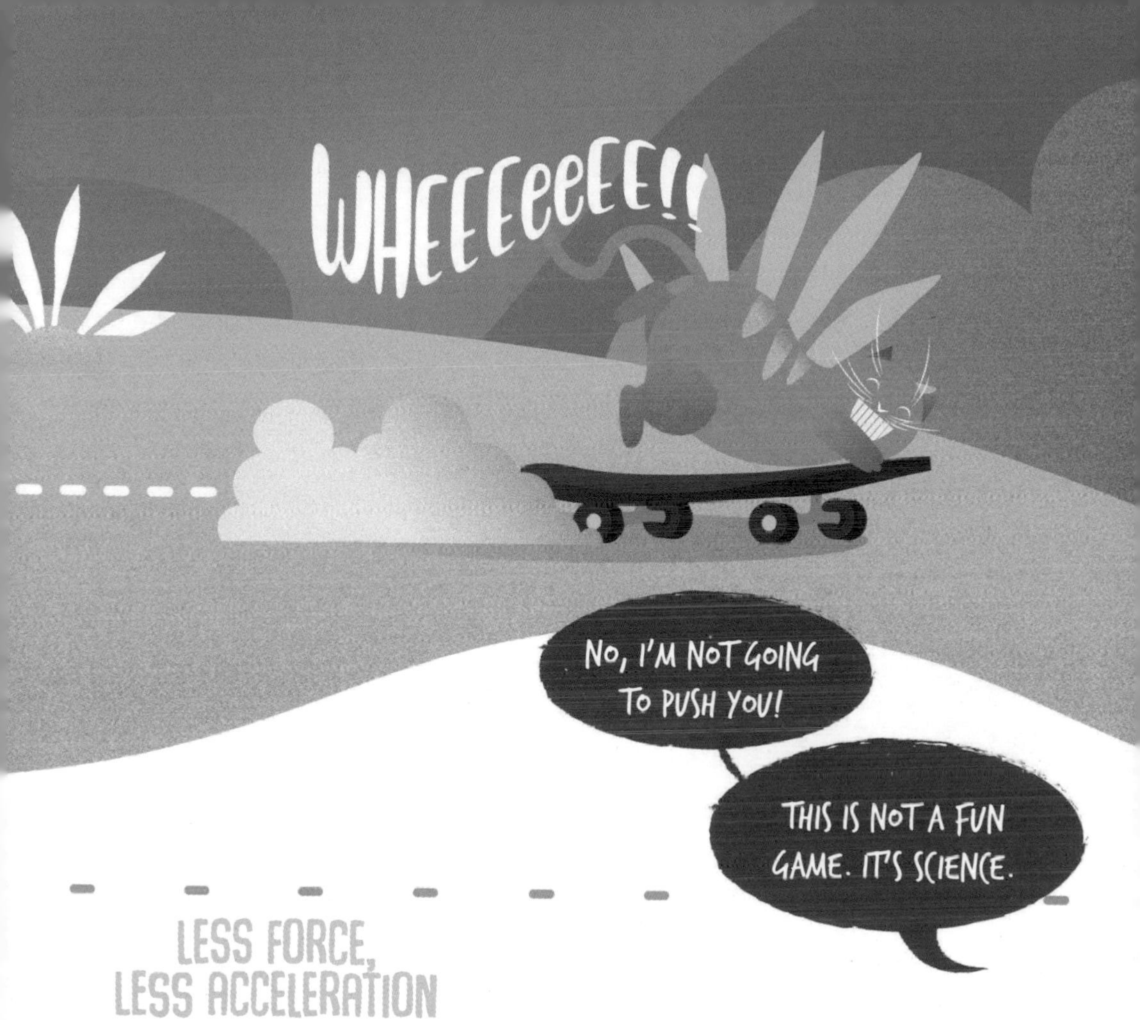


LESS FORCE,
LESS ACCELERATION

Newton's second law of motion says that the force acting on a thing depends on its mass and its acceleration..

FORCE

ELEPHANT CAMP

ACCELERATION

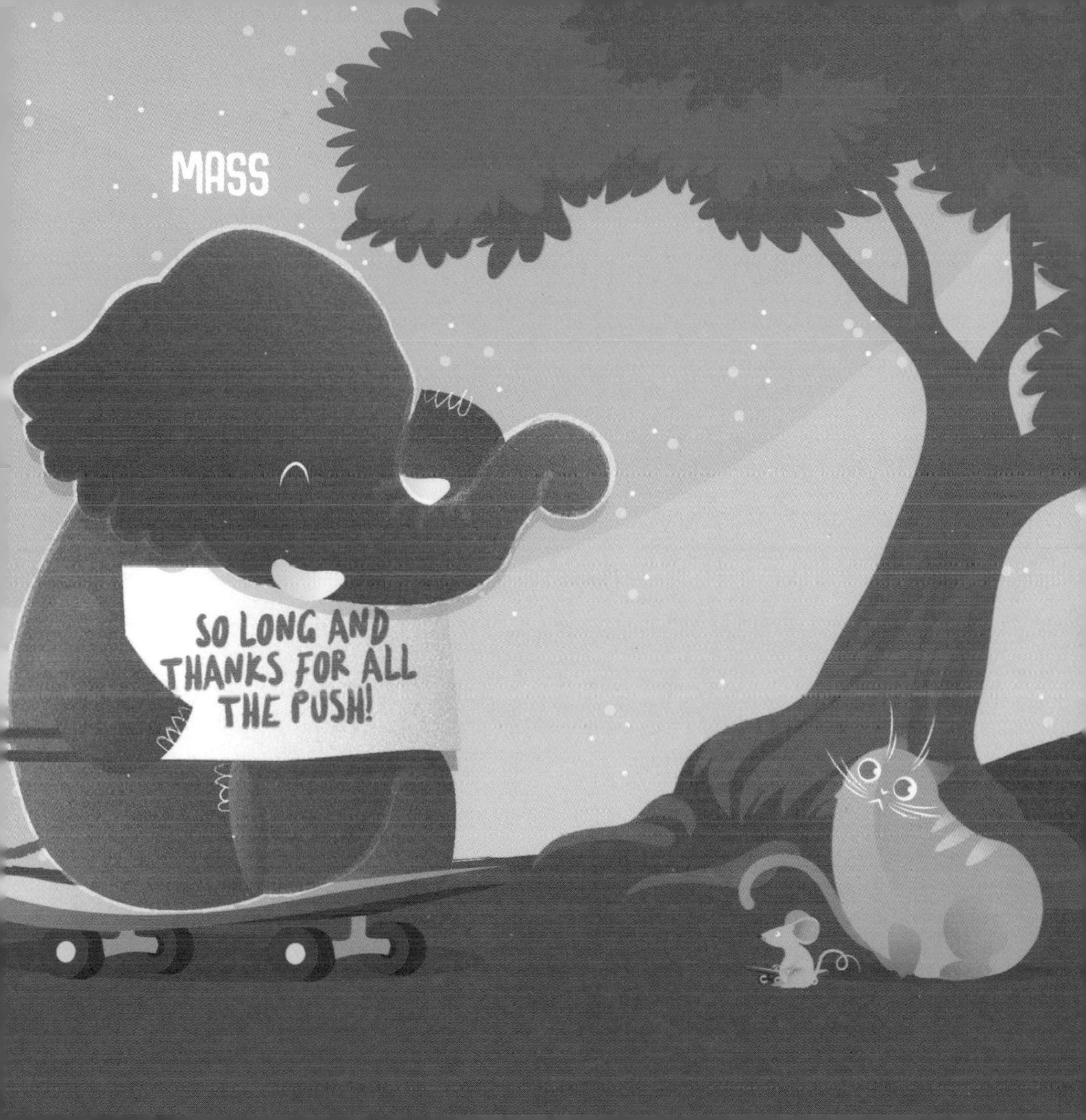
MASS
SO LONG AND THANKS FOR ALL THE PUSH!

When you put force on something, that thing also puts force on you.

When you pull the elephant, the elephant also pulls you.

When you pull the mouse, the mouse also pulls you. The force is less because the mass is less.

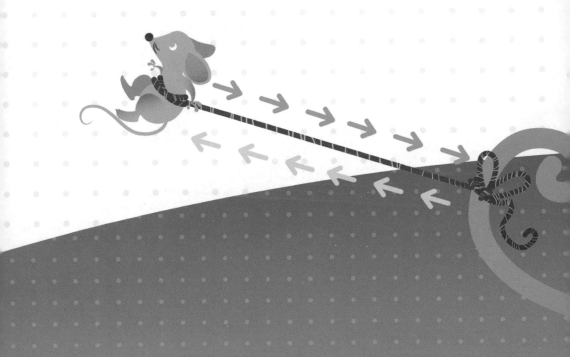

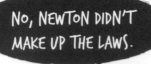

BECAUSE THEY ARE LAWS OF NATURE!
YES, OKAY, LAWS OF MOTION.
YES, SMARTYPANTS, YOU KNOW ALL ABOUT NEWTON'S LAWS OF MOTION NOW.

Anushka Ravishankar likes science, cats and books, not necessarily in that order. So she decided to write a book to explain science to a cat. The cat doesn't always get the point, but she hopes her readers will.

Pia Alizé Hazarika is an illustrator primarily interested in comics and visual narratives.

Her independent and collaborative work has been published by Penguin Random House India (*The PAO Anthology*), Comix India, Manta Ray Comics, The Pulpocracy, Captain Bijli Comics, Yoda Press, Zubaan Books and the Khoj Artists Collective. She runs PIG Studio, an illustration-driven space based out of New Delhi.

Her handle on Instagram is @_PigStudio_

## Read more in the series